Faith and Fitness:

6 Week Guide to Building a Healthy Life on a Foundation of Faith

Marsha Apsley, M.S.

Copyright © 2018 Marsha Apsley

All rights reserved.

Scripture taken from the New King James Version®. Copyright © 1982 by Thomas Nelson. Used by permission. All rights reserved.

Scripture quotations taken from the Amplified® Bible (AMP), Copyright © 2015 by The Lockman Foundation Used by permission. www.Lockman.org

ISBN: 1984373463
ISBN-13: 978-1984373465

CONTENTS

Welcome	i
About the Guide and the Journey	Pg 1
An Overview of my Philosophy	Pg 2
Faith	Pg 5
Food	Pg 9
Exercise	Pg 13
Water	Pg 16
Week 1	Pg 19
Week 2	Pg 23
Week 3	Pg 26
Week 4	Pg 30
Week 5	Pg 34
Week 6	Pg 39
Memory Verses	Pg 43
Epilogue	Pg 45
About the Author	Pg 47

WELCOME

Hello and Welcome! I'm so glad you are here.

For too long, I cried tears over the reflection in the mirror instead of seeing the woman God created me to be. For too long I was bound up with negative thoughts about myself and a focus on losing weight in order to be happy and feel good.

It is my prayer that no girl or woman struggle for as long as I did.

But even if you're 40+ years old (like I am), let me assure you that it is never too late to find freedom in Christ and embrace His unconditional love for you.

I now know that my healthy life must be built on a firm foundation of faith.

How is that done? By knowing God's Word and what He says about me and my body and then putting it into action. Some days it requires all the faith I have to believe I am "fearfully and wonderfully made" (see Psalm 139:14). Other days I get a glimpse that I truly am royalty and a daughter of a King.

Blessings on your journey! I'm praying for you and cheering you on.

xo,

Marsha

ABOUT THE GUIDE AND THE JOURNEY

Welcome to 6 Weeks of Faith and Fitness. This study guide is intended to take you on a six week journey that will help you build a healthy life on a firm foundation of faith. My devotional <u>40 Days of Faith and Fitness</u> (available on Amazon) would be a great companion for this guide as it will provide daily devotional content, a prayer, action step, and a page where you can journal. However, it is not required.

Each week you will have a memory verse* with some devotional content as well as a few questions to consider. These questions are intended for discussion with a friend or in a women's small group. You can certainly do it on your own, but I know from experience that I get so much more out of it when I discuss God's Word with others and have someone to hold me accountable.

*All memory verses available on the last page.
A few tips for memorizing scripture:
- Write it on a note card
- Say it out loud
- Post it where you can see it regularly, possibly on your computer or bathroom mirror
- Make it your screen saver or the wallpaper on your iphone

AN OVERVIEW OF MY PHILOSOPHY FOR A SUSTAINABLE HEALTHY LIFESTYLE

After working with dozens of women as well as being on my own healthy living journey, I've identified four areas — or pillars — for living a sustainable thriving life.

I've been on this journey my entire life, but unfortunately, I haven't always gone about it in a healthy way.

I consumed a lot of knowledge, became a certified Fitour group fitness instructor, followed Weight Watchers, loyally used Calorie King, and even went the Beachbody route for a while.

However, I got obsessive about all of it.

Finally I found some freedom from those numbers and specific plans, and I began to implement these four pillars in my life.

What I learned over time, along with the wisdom I gained from those I've worked with, is that focusing on these four areas daily can help us live a sustainable healthy life.

The 4 pillars are:
Faith ~ Food ~ Exercise ~ Water

Remember that you are unique, and it is important that you find how the implementation is going to look in *your own* life. It doesn't happen overnight, and it's more involved than saying a prayer, eating the right food, exercising and drinking water.

Take the time to learn what is best for your body:
- what the right food is for you
- what exercises you enjoy doing and the one(s) your body responds to
- what amount of water your body needs
- and faith. Faith is the most important piece to this puzzle, but it's one that is too often overlooked.

I want to stress that I am not perfect, and I certainly don't get it right all the time. But that's the thing: **a sustainable healthy life isn't one that's perfect. It's one that's livable.**

No more starting and stopping a plan or program. When you begin to implement these four pillars into your life, it will become a natural part of the way you live.

This guide is here to help you build on a firm foundation of faith, so you can finally feel the freedom you were meant to live *(see Galatians 5:1).*

Before we begin, let's take a look at those four areas in more detail.

FAITH

I believe that you have to have a firm foundation of faith for a lasting healthy lifestyle.

What I don't mean by needing a foundation of faith is this:
- Just pray to lose weight and you'll lose weight.
- Live by faith and you'll miraculously get fit and healthy without doing anything.
- It's necessary to be a member of a certain church to get healthy.

What I mean is this: In order to have a sustainable healthy lifestyle you must understand that it all starts on the inside. And it begins with what you believe about yourself, who you are, and how wonderfully and carefully you were created.

First some truths:
You have been fearfully and wonderfully made. (see Psalm 139:14)
You are loved. (see John 3:16)
Your body is a temple. (see 1 Corinthians 6:19)

How making faith part of your healthy lifestyle may look:

- *Read a daily devotion.* You can find a number of books in the library or online. You can sign up for a daily email. There are a number of apps that will pop up on your iphone and send you a reminder.
- *Listen to music.* Consider listening to Christian music. You might choose instrumental music.
- *Read scripture.* Simply open up your Bible and start reading.
- *Do a Bible study.* Again, you can find books that will lead you through one. There are a number of studies available online. Maybe you can join a small group at church.
- *Pray.*

This doesn't require a certain amount of time. Start with five minutes. The key is getting centered and grounded and focused. It's important to realize that there is more to healthy living than what we see on the outside.

You are more than a number on a scale or a dress size or a finish time.

This may be a new concept to you - considering faith part of your fitness. It took me a long time to understand that the Lord is interested in every single detail of my life. I served Him, but when it came to my body image struggles I figured a pill or plan could help with that. Then when it didn't, I cried all the tears feeling alone and helpless.

He patiently waited for me to realize I needed to lay it at His feet. Then I needed to believe, really believe, what He had to say about me. Most importantly, I had to take my healthy living plan and put it in perspective - no longer giving it all of my attention - and begin to wholly focus on Him.

I began to find freedom. I began to believe what He said about me. And I learned how to live a healthy lifestyle that was sustainable and got me results. Not some dramatic before and after picture, but freedom and peace.

Can I encourage you to address this very important part of your healthy living plan today?

Consider what I've written and ask yourself if you're putting too much emphasis on the outward appearance and not addressing the condition of your heart. Perhaps it's time to believe what He has said about you? Do you need to open your heart to His love and forgiveness in your life like I did?

FOOD

Food choices. For many this is our greatest struggle. Yes, we may be able to cut out sugar or carbs for a month, but we can't cut those things out forever. Some may find it easy to plan and pack meals for several weeks and then life happens and time gets cut short. Before you know it, the meals aren't packed and there's no dinner plan.

Making healthy food choices doesn't require a lot of time and energy. It doesn't need to be complicated. We're talking about a lifestyle here. We must come up with a way to eat that we can see ourselves doing a year from now and beyond.

Is this way of eating going to get you a bikini body in 30 days. Probably not. (But then again, what do you need for a bikini body? *Put a bikini on your body.* Okay, I digress.) We're looking for an effective way to eat that is also sustainable.

How do you eat so that it is healthy and sustainable and could even help you lose weight in the process?

First, you must become a detective. That starts by simply monitoring the food choices you're making right now. You may need to keep a food journal for a while. I'm not suggesting you count calories and become slave to a food list. But you don't know what you don't know. And the first thing you need to know is how you eat right now AND if it is serving you well.

As part of your detective work, monitor your food choices as well as how those foods are making you feel. When are you eating? Do you feel satisfied and energized by the way you eat? Or, are you always hungry? Do you suffer from the afternoon slump?

Answers to these questions will help you determine what foods are beneficial for your body *and* your schedule.

If you hear nothing else, please hear this: There is no one-size-fits-all way of eating. If someone tries to sell you an eating plan or program that is a photocopy of something he or she has sent to a dozen other people, then that is not going to work.

Once you begin to figure out patterns in your food choices and how you're feeling, then you can put together an eating plan that works for you.

Our bodies are smart. If we listen to them, they will let us know if a food is helpful to us or not.

Even the Bible has tips on how to eat.

1 Corinthians 10:31 tells us that *whatever we do, whether we eat or drink, we must do it for the glory of God.* And just a bit earlier in that same chapter, we read *"everything is permissible but not everything is beneficial"*.

This is basically saying "I can eat whatever I want, but I probably won't be doing myself any favors." Let's consider food allergies. I like peanuts and can't get enough peanut butter. It's perfectly fine for me to eat, and it satisfies me. Peanut butter is also permissible for the person who has a peanut allergy, but it isn't beneficial for her. That person must honor her unique body which, for whatever reason, cannot tolerate peanuts.

It does take some work to adopt a way of eating that is healthy and sustainable.

But once you do the work and establish your own priorities when it comes to the food choices that you make, you will be able to sustain that over the long term. We do things that make us feel good. So when we're feeding our bodies the nutrition that it needs, and we have the energy we need to live our daily lives, then we're going to stick with it.

EXERCISE

Exercise for a sustainable healthy lifestyle doesn't require running and biking and lifting and yoga. It doesn't require an hour at the gym six to seven days a week.

Exercise for a sustainable healthy lifestyle must be regular movement that you *like* to do, as well as regular movement that can fit into your schedule.

First, let's understand why is it important to exercise?

It's a great stress reliever.
It improves your confidence.
You'll sleep better.
It gives you more energy.
Contributes to weight loss if necessary.
It's good for your heart.

If you think you need to start running to get fit, but you hate running, you'll never stick with it. And if you start working out an hour a day every day of the week but you have kids in activities and a job that requires 40+ hours a week, you won't stick with that workout.

Recently, I ran a 6 mile race on Saturday and a 5K race on Sunday. I don't often do two races in a weekend, but I did this time because I forgot I had signed up for one of them. Oops! I had to take it easy on both, because I'd had a bit of an injury I didn't want to aggravate.

But doing two races, or even one in a weekend, may not excite you in the least. And that's okay. Let's find out what does.

Do you like to dance? Try Zumba or turn on the music at home and have a dance party for one!

Do you like to walk? Walking is a FANTASTIC way to exercise.

Do you like to lift heavy things? Lifting is good for bone health and metabolism.

Do you want to focus more on stretching and de-stressing? Try yoga.

Do you need variety in your life? Pick a few things to do.

The key to this is doing *something*. Move. Get outside and get some fresh air. Start with a walk around the block. Grab a friend and try a new class. I think you'll find that you enjoy it and that you feel better when you do it.

Next consider how much time you have. Do you have 10 or 15 minutes? Then you have time to fit in some exercise. It doesn't require an hour everyday.

WATER

Some people will tell you eight glasses a day. Others say drink a gallon of water.

I've landed in the middle and suggest you drink half your body weight in ounces of water. Last time I had a scale I was in the 150 range, so I shoot for 75 ounces of water daily. I also like this method, because I firmly believe that your health and fitness is very unique to you. Therefore basing *your* water intake on *your* weight makes your daily water requirement another reminder that you have to do you! Eight glasses of water a day might work for your 130 pound friend. A large active male may shoot for a gallon of water a day.

But how much should *you* drink? Focus on you.

I think we know many of the benefits of drinking water....

It fills you up to aid in suppressing appetite.
It keeps things moving smoothly. (And that's all I'll say about that ☐)
It flushes out toxins.
It helps regulate body temperature.
It's good for your skin.

When I taught step aerobics years ago, I had a gal in my class replace her daily soda with water. With that change alone she lost several pounds!

When you add water to your daily intake, you often replace something else and usually it's something that wasn't beneficial to begin with like that sugary soda or flavored coffee.

If you don't drink much of anything at all and add water to your daily routine, you will notice increased energy. You will likely hit the restroom more often but that's good because it's flushing out the bad stuff.

You see, water doesn't make you bloat. You bloat when your body is trying to hold onto water, because it thinks it's not going to get more of it.

Establishing a sustainable healthy lifestyle doesn't require a bunch of huge changes all at once. Increasing your water intake is a good place to begin. Like mentioned earlier, your energy will increase. If you feel bloated, you may see some relief from that. It will help curb your appetite. It's a great starting point.

Now let's get on with the study!

WEEK 1

Memory Verse: *"Present your bodies a living sacrifice, holy, acceptable to God, which is your reasonable service."*
Romans 12:1 (NKJV)

At the beginning of any journey, we must set a focus.

If we want to build our healthy lives on a firm foundation of faith, we must be ready to say "Here I am Lord, do in me as You please."

This scripture reminds us that we are His, and we must present ourselves to Him.

Verse 2 goes on to say *"And do not be conformed to this world, but be transformed by the renewing of your mind, that you may prove what is that good and acceptable and perfect will of God."*

Faith and fitness

As you embark on this journey to establish a fit and healthy life, I want you to understand the importance of building on a foundation of faith.

Without Him we can do nothing.

Without Him what we do is in vain.

He created us with a physical body, and He wants us to take care of ourselves. (We'll talk more about that in the weeks to come.) But we can't give the physical priority over our spiritual life. This verse shows us how we can do this in a way pleasing to Him......*present our bodies to Him.*

"And do not be conformed to this world"

The diets, gimmicks, and quick fixes. We have to say **No** to them and **Yes** to His direction in our lives.

When we do this, we then begin to see and live out His *"acceptable and perfect will"* in our lives.

This week is all about committing the process to Him. It's about being willing to do fitness *His way.* That means appreciating where we are in our lives right now, learning how to honor that, and living it out as an act of worship to our Creator.

Discussion Questions

Are you ready to approach your fitness journey with a faith focus?

How will you present yourself to God this week?

What diets and gimmicks have you tried in the past that just didn't seem to work?

What thoughts will you have to replace as you start to do fitness in a different way?

WEEK 2

Memory Verse: *"So whether you eat or drink or whatever you do, do it all for the glory of God."* 1 Corinthians 10:31 (NKJV)

Whatever you do…no matter what it is, do it for God's glory.

The scripture is clear that all that we do, every action that we take, should be for the glory of God.

If you read my blog or follow me on social media, you'll notice there is a lot of focus on fitness and on healthy living. And the reason I love this verse is that it specifically states *"whether you eat or drink"* - God is interested in that.

When I overindulge, is that glorifying God?

When I don't take care of what I put into my body, does that glorify God?

When I hit snooze several times and then get up in a rush and start my day frazzled, does that glorify God?

We've been entrusted with one life - one body. We are to use it to glorify Him.

As we move through this week, let's become more aware of the things we are eating and drinking and ask ourselves if what we are putting into our bodies and how we are treating our bodies is glorifying to God.

As you reflect on this verse, know that the reason it's important is that He loves you and me so much that He wants us to invite Him into *every part* of our lives.

Discussion Questions

How can you become more aware of the things you are eating and drinking?

What might you need to change about your daily life to bring more glory to God?

Would God be pleased if He sat down at the table with us?

WEEK 3

Memory Verse: *"Therefore, since we are surrounded by such a great cloud of witnesses, let us throw off everything that hinders and the sin that so easily entangles. And let us run with perseverance the race marked out for us,"* Hebrews 12:1 **(NIV)**

Yes, I'm a runner. No, I won't be asking you to run this week!

There is so much we can take from this verse to apply to our journey of fitness.

There are 2 parts of this verse I want to focus on this week:

1. let us throw off everything that hinders us
2. let us run...the race marked out for us

"let us throw off everything that hinders"

Before we can get going in the race, we must throw off everything that hinders us.

Think about an action-packed movie you've watched where there is a water rescue. The first thing the hero does is start peeling off his clothes. (Now now, I'm not trying to sidetrack you with this hot guy hero image!)

Here's the thing - before the hero can jump into the water and make the rescue, he takes off all the extra baggage that would hinder him from making a safe rescue.

It's the same with us.

We want to get going on our journey and make progress. We want to be successful as we move towards the goals that we've set.

But first, we have to get rid of the things that are holding us back and weighing us down.

From personal experience and from my work with women along the way, often I find that the thing hindering us the most is the way we think. We are held captive by negative thoughts, poor body image, beliefs we grabbed onto years ago and continue to hold onto today.

We must go through this part of the process before we can move forward.

"let us run...the race marked out for us"

We're not running just *any* race, we're running *our* race - the race marked out for us.

You are running the race marked for you. I'm running the race marked out for me. (Or we *should* be.)

Too often you and I get caught up in running someone else's race.

In our fitness journey, we do this by trying a diet that worked for our friend or drinking the shake that helped our sister lose the weight, or eating the way the girl on social media eats.

This is where keeping our eyes on our own paper comes in.

We can't run our race well if we're trying to mimic what someone else is doing. Even if something works for someone else, it may not work for you. Why? Because she's not you!

Only you are you!

When we waste our time doing what someone else is doing, we're making our own journey longer and more difficult.

We can't live somebody else's life. We won't get somebody else's results.

We must live the life that we've been given. There are so many unique factors to each of our lives.

Trying to do life like someone else only distracts and detours us. It slows us down and impedes our progress.

Discussion Questions

How is our fitness journey like running a race?

What things do you need to throw off that might be hindering you from moving forward?

Have you tried to run someone else's race or go at her pace? How did that work out?

WEEK 4

Memory Verse: *"Do you not know that your bodies are temples of the Holy Spirit, who is in you, whom you have received from God? You are not your own; you were bought at a price. Therefore honor God with your bodies."* 1 Corinthians 6:19-20 (NIV)

When you think of a temple, what comes to mind?

For me, it's a huge cathedral I've only seen pictures of. I think of Roman cathedrals and large churches.

What are you picturing right now?

If we align this with our verse for the week, it makes me stop and think about who I am.

Do you not know? Don't you know - YOU are a temple!

I sense a great deal of emphasis here. It feels like somebody is taking me and shaking me and saying "Marsha, don't you know you're a temple?? Start living like it!"

You and I are not our own. Christ paid for us. He values us. It's time for us to start looking at our reflection with the same awe and wonder that we look at those huge cathedrals and temples we only see in pictures.

Let's settle our thoughts on this truth today: **We are a temple.**

If we can agree that we are a temple, that our bodies are a temple, then we are going to care for them differently. We're not going to fill our bodies with trash, junk food or the scraps left on our children's plates.

Please don't misunderstand. I'm not saying that you have to cut out all the sugar, pizza, burgers, cocktails, etc.

What I'm saying is that we should be mindful of what we are putting into our bodies. We must be aware of the choices we are making and if they are honoring our body in a healthy way.

Go to the mirror and say to that reflection "I am a temple. You {insert your name here} are a temple."

Discussion Questions

Can you look at yourself like a temple? What unique details stand out to you?

Can you identify traits and qualities about you and your body that you are grateful for?

Are you caring for your body more like a temple or a trash can?

What changes might you make to better care for your body?

WEEK 5

Memory Verse: *"Everything is permissible, but not everything is beneficial."* 1 Corinthians 10:23 (AMP)

There you have it.

We can have, eat, drink, do whatever we want, *but* it's not all beneficial. In some cases, it's quite clear what is beneficial. In other cases, not so much.

According to dictionary.com, <u>permissible</u> is that which is allowed. Some other ways to define it is what's tolerable, or basically what is all right.

Looking back at the verse, it's simply saying everything is all right. Anything is allowable in your life.

It's all right to eat chicken and vegetables.

It's all right to eat pizza and drink Coke.

It's all right to lay around all day everyday.

It's all right to run and walk and play.

Are you getting my point?

You could come up with as many sentences as there are foods, activities, etc. and you could say "It's all right to do X, Y, Z."

However, there is a *but*.

And that is where the work starts. It's the part following the *but*.

If everything was permissible and it stopped there, I don't think we would like the results.

And yet, sometimes we live our day to day lives denying what is behind the *but*...the beneficial part...and living like it's all okay.

I think we can agree that even though it might *sound* good to be able to eat, drink, have, do whatever we want, it wouldn't make for a very good life experience.

How do we decide what is beneficial?

This is where the work comes in.

This is where *you* have to do *you*.

This means listening to your body and taking notes on how it feels after you eat certain things.

Does this food leave me feeling like I want to eat more?

Does it leave me feeling energized or sluggish?

Does this exercise hurt my body or make me feel better when I finish?

It's these kinds of questions we must begin to consider when we ask ourselves "Is this beneficial?"

And here's the key: Nobody can answer these questions for you.

So, keep your eyes on your own paper and start taking notes.

Be your own detective!

When I looked up beneficial in the Thesaurus, one of the phrases was "what the doctor ordered." We usually follow through with the doctor's orders, because we trust him and his experience.

To figure out what is beneficial takes work. It takes time. It takes trusting and honoring the feedback we get from our own body. We will try, and we will fail. It's part of the process. But that's how we learn and make changes and find the right formula.

Eating and drinking and moving is something we will do for the rest of our lives.

To think that in one week or even one month we'll get it figured out is limiting our progress.

How? Because when we don't see the results we think we should in that week or month, we totally give up. When you stop being a detective and listening to your body, then you go back to yo-yo diets and poor body image and negative beliefs and all the things that didn't work in the past.

Let's commit to the process and learn what is beneficial for us.

Discussion Questions

How would life be if there was not a *but* in this verse?

How will you decide what is beneficial for your body?

Are you willing to do some detective work to figure it out?

What are you afraid of if you begin to listen to your own body and do what works for you?

WEEK 6

Memory Verse: *"I will praise You, for I am fearfully and wonderfully made; marvelous are Your works, and that my soul knows very well."* Psalm 139:14 (NKJV)

This is our last week but the journey is one that will continue through all our days.

We began this journey by presenting ourselves to Him, completely, fully.

My prayer is that we are ending this knowing that we are perfect in His sight.

No matter where you are on the journey, He loves you. I hope that you can praise Him for the way that He has made you.

He is satisfied with us when we come to Him. He wants us to come to Him with praise for Who He is and who He has made us to be.

Yes, He wants us to be good stewards of these bodies and this life He has entrusted to us.

We've read scripture that clearly shows us that we are to honor Him by honoring our bodies. That is something we can commit to every single day for the rest of our lives.

No matter where you are on this healthy living journey, He wants to continue walking with you. He wants you to give each and every day to Him. He is there to give you strength to obey His word and to live out the life He has designed for you to live.

Although this is the end of our journey, may it be for you the beginning of a life lived in freedom with your eyes only looking to Jesus.

Discussion Questions

What progress have you made over the last 6 weeks? Spiritually? Physically?

How has your thinking about yourself changed?

How has your approach to healthy living changed?

What are your takeaways?

MEMORY VERSES

"Present your bodies a living sacrifice, holy, acceptable to God, which is your reasonable service." Romans 12:1 (NKJV)

"So whether you eat or drink or whatever you do, do it all for the glory of God." 1 Corinthians 10:31 (NKJV)

"Therefore, since we are surrounded by such a great cloud of witnesses, let us throw off everything that hinders and the sin that so easily entangles. And let us run with perseverance the race marked out for us," Hebrews 12:1 (NIV)

"Do you not know that your bodies are temples of the Holy Spirit, who is in you, whom you have received from God? You are not your own; you were bought at a price. Therefore honor God with your bodies." 1 Corinthians 6:19-20 (NIV)

"Everything is permissible, but not everything is beneficial." 1 Corinthians 10:23 (AMP)

"I will praise You, for I am fearfully and wonderfully made; marvelous are Your works, and that my soul knows very well." Psalm 139:14 (NKJV)

Marsha Apsley

EPILOGUE

Dear Sister,

Thank you for going on this journey. Please do not view this as the end but the beginning of a life lived in freedom in Christ.

He loves you so much and does not want you to go back to a life of questions and doubts. He doesn't want for you a life of diet roller coasters and striving to fit into society's mold.

He wants you to thrive in the life He has designed for you.

He doesn't require that we get it right all the time but only that we keep our eyes on Him and commit to moving forward on the path He has laid out for us.

I'm still on the journey and will be until He calls me home. I desire to live out what He is teaching me along the way about building my fit life on a foundation of faith. I commit to sharing that with women like you who desire to do the same.

Yours in faith and fitness,

Marsha

46

ABOUT THE AUTHOR

Marsha is a counselor and is passionate about helping women live fit and free. She does this by focusing on whole person health and wellness with an emphasis on how women feel about themselves. She believes that a healthy lifestyle needs to be built on a firm foundation of faith. She is committed to helping you take a faith-based approach to living your best life.

She is a wife and mom of two sons. She loves to run and bike and enjoy a cup of coffee with friends. For more support and encouragement on your faith and fitness journey, please visit her website www.marshaapsley.com or find her on social media @marshaapsley or email marsha@marshaapsley.com

Made in the USA
Monee, IL
22 August 2024

64319237R00030